Introduction

A good book can touch our lives like a good friend. Within its pages are words and characters that can inspire us to achieve our highest ideals. We can turn to it for companionship, recreation, comfort, and guidance. It also gives us a cherished story to hold in our hearts forever.

In *Literature Units*, great care has been taken to select books that are sure to become good friends!

Teachers who use this unit will find the following features to supplement their own valuable ideas.

- Sample Lesson Plans

- Pre-reading Activities

- Biographical Sketch and Picture of the Author

- Book Summary

- Vocabulary Lists and Suggested Vocabulary Activities

- Chapters grouped for study, with sections including the following:

    — a quiz

    — a hands-on project

    — a cooperative learning activity

    — a cross-curriculum connection

    — an extension into the reader's own life

- Post-reading Activities

- Book Report Ideas

- Research Ideas

- Culminating Activities

- Three Options for Unit Tests

- Bibliography of Related Reading

- Answer Key

We are confident that this unit will be a valuable addition to your planning, and we hope that as you use our ideas, your students will increase the circle of friends they have in books.

Sample Lesson Plan

Lesson 1
- Introduce and complete some of the pre-reading activities (page 5).
- Read About the Author with students (page 6).
- Introduce vocabulary words for Section 1 (page 8).

Lesson 2
- Read Chapters 1–5. As you read, place the vocabulary words in the context of the story and discuss their meanings (page 8).
- Do a Vocabulary Activity (page 9).
- Share facts about Egypt (page 13) with students.
- As a class, complete the map of Egypt (page 11) to give students a sense of the geography of the place the book is describing.
- Begin Character Ads (page 12).
- Begin constructing Egypt in the classroom (page 14).
- Administer Section 1 Quiz (page 10).
- Introduce vocabulary words for Section 2 (page 8).

Lesson 3
- Read Chapters 6–9. Place the vocabulary words in the context of the story and discuss their meanings (page 8).
- Do a Vocabulary Activity (page 9).
- Continue Character Ads for new characters introduced in this section (page 12).
- Complete Shopping for Egypt activity (page 18).
- Continue constructing Egypt in the classroom (page 14).
- Fill out the Police Report (page 17).
- Create a Pharaoh (page 16).
- Make a costume for an Egyptian (page 20).
- Administer Section 2 Quiz (page 15).
- Introduce vocabulary words for Section 3 (page 8).

Lesson 4
- Read Chapters 10–14. Place vocabulary words in the context of the story and discuss their meanings (page 8).
- Do a Vocabulary Activity (page 9).

- Complete Egyptian Analogies (page 24).
- Introduce Hieroglyphics alphabet (page 22).
- Create Hieroglyph necklaces (page 25).
- Break the Hieroglyphic code (page 23).
- Administer Section 3 Quiz (page 21).
- Introduce vocabulary words for Section 4 (page 8).

Lesson 5
- Read Chapters 15–19. Place vocabulary words in the context of the story and discuss their meanings (page 8).
- Do a Vocabulary Activity (page 9).
- Create Questions for the Oracle (page 28).
- Complete To Ask or Not? (page 29).
- Sequence the "Ceremony for the Dead" (page 30).
- Write a letter about a lost friend (page 27).
- Administer Section 4 Quiz (page 26).
- Introduce vocabulary words for Section 5 (page 8).

Lesson 6
- Read Chapters 20–23. Place vocabulary words in the context from the story and discuss their meanings (page 8).
- Introduce words from ancient Egypt (page 32).
- Make and play vocabulary guessing game (page 32).
- Use Internet resources to learn facts about pyramids (page 35).
- Complete Key Clues math (page 34).
- Administer Section 5 Quiz (page 31).
- Create Egypt Game game board (page 33).

Lesson 7
- Discuss Newbury Award books (page 36).
- Assign book report and research projects (pages 37 and 38).
- Do a Culminating Activity (pages 39–42).

Lesson 8
- Administer Unit Test 1, 2, and/or 3 (pages 43–45).
- Do another Culminating Activity (page 39–42).

A Guide for Using

The Egypt Game

in the Classroom

*Based on the novel written
by Zilpha Keatley Snyder*

*This guide written by **Kelli Plaxco***

Teacher Created Materials, Inc.
6421 Industry Way
Westminster, CA 92683
www.teachercreated.com
©2001 Teacher Created Materials, Inc.
Made in U.S.A.
ISBN-0-7439-3006-1

Edited by
Karen Tam Froloff

Illustrated by
Howard Chaney

Cover Art by
Wendy Chang

Table of Contents

Before the Book

Before you begin reading *The Egypt Game* with your students, do some pre-reading activities to stimulate interest and enhance comprehension. Here are some activities that might work well in your class.

1. Predict what the story might be about by hearing the title.

2. Predict what the story might be about by looking at the cover.

3. Point out the Newbery Medal that *The Egypt Game* won. Talk about how a book receives this award and have the students brainstorm a list of other Newbery Award winners they have read. See explanation and list on page 36.

4. Discuss other books about Egypt that the students may have read or heard about.

5. Provide each student with a copy of the facts about Egypt (page 13). This will familiarize them with the terminology used in Egypt's past and will also stimulate any prior knowledge they may have about Egypt.

6. Ask students the following questions:

   • What do you imagine it would be like to live with your grandmother?

   • What would it be like to have a mother who was a movie star, but she was so busy that you hardly ever got to see her? Talk about the advantages and the disadvantages.

   • Do you think it is alright to use another person's property if that person does not ever use it? Explain your view.

   • How many of you ever had a special toy, doll, or blanket that you took with you everywhere you went or that you slept with every night? Did you ever lose that item? And if so, how did you feel?

7. Discuss what you think it would have been like to live in Egypt during the time that the pyramids were being built.

About the Author

Three-time Newbery Honor Book award recipient, Zilpha Keatley Snyder, was born on May 11, 1928, in southern California. It is here where she also spent most of her childhood. Born into a family with three daughters during the years of the Great Depression, Zilpha did not have much by way of material possessions or opportunities. As a result, young Zilpha's life during that time mostly revolved around animals and books.

Zilpha began reading at a very young age and she loved to read all of the time. One of her fondest childhood memories was the day the public librarian issued her a library card. All throughout school, she developed a passion for the written word, reading an average of seven or eight books every week.

At the age of eight, Zilpha decided to become a writer and even at this tender age, knew that this was the profession that would last her a lifetime. Zilpha had visions of graduating from college and then going on to live in an attic somewhere to write and/or to starve. Once she began writing, she continued to write for the next 13 years. Her works during that time included poems, short stories, and many unfinished novels.

As Zilpha prepared to graduate from college, she married Larry Snyder. After their wedding, they moved to New York so that he could acquire his master's degree in music. While he attended graduate school, Zilpha worked as a public school teacher. Throughout the next several years, she traveled, taught school, and raised three children.

But it was the year that Zilpha's youngest child entered school that marked a turning point in her career—a renewed interest in writing. With nine years of teaching behind her, Zilpha pursued writing again, but this time, she focused her writing on literature for children. Her first book, *Season of Ponies*, was published in 1964.

Since that day many years ago, Zilpha has written many other works for children. Most of her books were inspired by events that happened in her own life. The children she taught in California inspired the story for *The Egypt Game* while some troubles in her son's life were the inspiration for *Black and Blue Magic*.

The Newbery Medal is one of the greatest honors given to a piece of children's literature and in 1968, *The Egypt Game* was an honor book for the Newbery Medal. Zilpha Keatley Snyder has also won Newbery Honor Book awards for two of her other books, *The Witches of Worm* in 1973 and *The Headless Cupid* in 1972.

The Egypt Game

by Zilpha Keatley Snyder
(Bantam Doubleday Dell Books for Young Readers, 1967)

(Available in Canada, Doubleday Dell Seal; UK, Bantam Doubleday Dell; AUS, Transworld Publishing)

The Egypt Game tells the story of April Hall and her adventures as she moves in with her grandmother. She is forced to leave behind a life of what she sees as "glamour and movie stars." She must replace those things in her life with a different place that seems to have nothing to offer. Then she meets Melanie Ross, a young girl the same age as her, who lives in the same apartment complex.

After spending only one afternoon together, they quickly learn that they both like to play what they call "imagining games." Those imagining games are what lead the pair to the creation of "The Egypt Game."

One afternoon, they stumble upon a deserted storage yard behind the A-Z Antique and Curio Shop. After investigating the contents of the yard, they decide it reminds them of ancient Egypt. The two girls, along with Melanie's little brother, use all of their knowledge about the civilizations of ancient Egypt to transform this deserted old yard into a place where a High Priestess, or even a Pharaoh, would go.

They create their own hieroglyphics alphabet, their own ceremonial traditions, and their own private place where Egyptian culture comes alive. This mysterious place does not stay private for long as the number of "Egyptians" in their little group grows from three to six.

The six Egyptians meet in the deserted yard every chance they get and even use their hieroglyphics alphabet to pass secret messages in school. "The Egypt Game" is becoming a part of their daily lives. That is, until something terrible happens in their neighborhood, something that causes all of the parents in the area to keep their children at home. After this tragic event, the Egyptians fear that "The Egypt Game" may be lost forever.

What today's society has discovered about ancient Egyptian civilization has shown that these people were full of mystery and intrigue. Their hierarchical society and ceremonial rituals have fascinated people of the modern world for many years. Zilpha Keatley Snyder takes the reader into the same mysterious world, page by page, as "The Egypt Game" is played.

Vocabulary Lists

On this page are vocabulary lists that correspond to each sectional group of chapters. Vocabulary activities can be found on page 9 in this book.

Section 1: Chapters 1–5

Nefertiti	evasive	petrified	Syrians
pharaoh	heir	reincarnation	corrugated
hieroglyphics	escapades	monoliths	dead-pan

Section 2: Chapters 6–9

rituals	sinister	processions	tunics
incense	Cleopatra	papyrus	chaperoned
medley	dutifully	languishing	summoned

Section 3: Chapters 10–14

liable	prostrated	trance-like	angular
convulsions	fiendish	humanity	warily
omen	philosophically	diplomacy	

Section 4: Chapters 15–19

rendezvous	grottoes	solemn	spectator
populace	pilgrimage	oracle	
brine	dahlias	consternation	

Section 5: Chapters 20–23

rasped	alabaster	gloat	Egyptologist
alibi	primitive	exasperated	anthropology
bewildered	province	seclusion	gypsies

Vocabulary Activities

You can help your students learn and retain the vocabulary in *The Egypt Game* by providing them with interesting vocabulary activities. Here are a few ideas to try.

❑ As the students read each section, encourage them to use the vocabulary words from those chapters to play **Vocabulary Concentration**. The goal of this game is to match vocabulary words with their definitions. To play the game, divide the class into pairs. Have students make two sets of cards that are the same size, but two different colors. On one colored set, they will write the vocabulary words (one word per card). On the second set, they will write the definitions (one definition per card). All of the cards are mixed together and then laid in rows face down on a table. A player picks two cards, one of each color and then reads the word and definition. If they are a match, the player keeps the two cards. If they are not a match, the player turns them back over and his or her turn is over. The game continues until all matches have been made.

❑ Challenge students to a **Vocabulary Bee**. This is similar to a Spelling Bee, but in addition to spelling the word correctly, the game participants must define the words, as well. This could be done with the teacher or a designated student as the moderator.

❑ Ask students to write **Creative Paragraphs**, using the vocabulary words for each section. The only rule is that their paragraph must be a story that has Egypt as its setting. This is a chance for the students' creative juices to flow as they re-create Egypt as they imagine it.

❑ Challenge students to use a specific vocabulary word from the section at least **Ten Times in One Day**. They must keep a record of when, how, and why the word was used. At the end of the day, have the students trade record sheets with each other and see if the partners agree with how the students used the vocabulary word.

❑ Play **Twenty Questions** with the entire class. In this game, one student selects a vocabulary word and gives clues about the word, such as the part of speech the word is, the number of syllables it has, etc. The clues should be given one by one until someone in the class guesses the word. The only thing is that whoever guesses the word has to define it!

❑ **Vocabulary Comics** are a fun way to reinforce the words. Have students select 8–9 words from each section. Ask them to create a comic strip with an Egyptian theme that uses the words in the dialogue. Provide copies of your local newspaper's comic section to give them a variety of pattern choices.

❑ Have students practice their alphabetizing skills in **ABC Drill** by dividing the class into groups of three or four. Each group writes one vocabulary word per card from the first group of words. On a given signal, tell students to alphabetize the word cards. When the group has completed the task, they quickly and quietly stand up. The first group to finish is declared the winner. Each sectional group of words can be added as the book is read.

❑ In **Scrambled Vocabulary**, students write a sentence using each vocabulary word. The letters in the vocabulary word are mixed up when written in the sentence. Students then exchange papers and unscramble their partner's vocabulary words using the context clues from the sentence.

Quiz Time

1. On the back of this paper, list three main events from this section. Then write one sentence to describe what you predict will happen in the next section.

2. Describe how you see the relationship between April and her grandmother.

   _____

   _____

3. What made the girls start thinking about Egypt?

   _____

   _____

4. Why did people think of the Professor as "dangerous"?

   _____

   _____

5. When April met Melanie, she was wearing a fur stole, fake eyelashes, and her hair was in a sweep. Why to you think she dressed this way?

   _____

   _____

6. In what month did the girls start "The Egypt Game"?

   _____

   _____

7. In the chapter, "Enter Melanie and Marshall," April and Melanie talk about playing "imagining games" like the paper doll families. Name two "imagining" games that you know of.

   _____

   _____

8. Where did April and her grandmother live?

   _____

   _____

9. How did Melanie and April convince Marshall to play the game with them?

   _____

   _____

10. How old was the item that April found in the A-Z Antique and Curio Shop?

   _____

   _____

The Geography of Egypt

Use the Internet, as well as other available classroom resources (i.e., atlas, encyclopedia, etc.), to help you complete this map of Egypt.

Label the following geographical items.		
1. Cairo	6. Mediterranean Sea	11. Gulf of Suez
2. Red Sea	7. Suez	12. Sinai Peninsula
3. Nile River	8. Suez Canal	13. Israel
4. Alexandria	9. Sudan	14. Gulf of Aqaba
5. Aswan	10. Libya	15. Al Minya

Character Ads

Use this activity throughout the novel as new characters are introduced.

Bring in a copy of your local newspaper's personal ads section to give to students. This will serve as an example of how personal ads sometimes read. Then give each student a stack of approximately 16–20 3" x 5" (8 cm x 13 cm) index cards. You could also cut your own cards from tagboard.

Decide ahead of time if you want to include all of the characters or just the main ones. Every time the author introduces a new character, students will need two cards—one for the character's name and one for his or her personal ad. Encourage students to write four or five clues about each person. The first clue should start as a more general description and then progress to more detailed clues. Conclude with a very specific clue that could only fit that character. See example below.

April Hall

- one of the six Egyptians
- has a great imagination
- very stubborn
- likes to create Egyptian ceremonies
- misses her mother very much

After students create the two cards for each character, they will need to keep the cards all together until the end of the unit. These cards can be used in several ways as follows:

1. Have the students turn in the cards for a grade on character descriptions.

2. Have students divide into pairs, trade cards with each other, and try to match their partner's character cards with the correct description.

3. Have each pair of students use a set of cards from a different pair of students to play "Character Concentration." This is played in the same way as Vocabulary Concentration on page 9.

4. Divide the class into two teams and gather up everyone's personal ad cards. The teacher will choose one card from the pile and begin writing its phrases on the board, one at a time. After the teacher writes one clue, each team guesses who the character is. If neither team guesses correctly, the teacher continues to add a clue until one team guesses the correct character.

Facts You Should Know About Egypt

Teacher Suggestion: Use the following facts for research and discussion.

◆ Egypt is an Arab nation located in northern Africa.

◆ The capital city, Cairo, is the most populous city in Africa and among the Arab nations.

◆ Egyptian civilization dates back to over 6,000 years ago.

◆ Most of the ancient Egyptian civilization had their existence along the Nile River. They were considered to be one of the first agricultural societies.

◆ The Nile River is the longest river in the world. It is about 4,145 miles (6,669 km) long. Its source is in Lake Victoria and it flows northward to the Mediterranean Sea.

◆ Today, 99% of Egypt's people live along the Nile River or near the Suez Canal.

◆ The Pharaoh, or Egyptian king, led the ancient Egyptian civilization. Most Pharaohs were men, but a few of the well-known pharoahs were women, such as Cleopatra and Nefertiti.

◆ The Great Pyramids are considered to be one of the Seven Ancient Wonders of the World, and you can still visit them today in Egypt. They were built as tombs to house and protect the body of a Pharoah for the after life.

◆ Mummification was practiced by the Egyptians to preserve the body in the pyramids so that it did not decay.

◆ Egyptians believed that one of their most important gods, Osiris, the god of death and resurrection, was the first to be mummified.

◆ Egyptians wrote with signs called hieroglyphics instead of using an alphabet of letters. Many of these signs were a kind of picture of what sound they represented.

◆ Papyrus was a plant Egyptians used to make the first known type of writing paper.

Constructing Egypt in Your Classroom

As the story of *The Egypt Game* unfolds, students can create their own "Egypt" in the classroom, much like April and Melanie did in the backyard of the A-Z Antique and Curio Shop. Use the bibliography on page 46 to provide the students with resource books to look at as they begin designing their "Egypt." Students could do this as a whole-class activity, or divide them into two or three groups and give each group a corner of the classroom to use. As the book comes to an end and their "Egypt" is completed, give each group an opportunity to present it to the class, or to a visiting class of students. Students can talk about how their "Egypt" is similar and/or different from the one that the author created in the readers' minds. They can also distinguish between the items that they feel are true replications from ancient Egyptian society, and the ones they created themselves that they think could have been a part of this culture.

Students can use the diagram below as a springboard to get them started. Egypt Area # 1, for example, could include a statue of Nefertiti, an incense burning bird bath, a rug for laying prostate, and a holy water bird bath. As students read the story, they will all have their own ideas of how they see Zilpha Keatley Snyder's "Egypt." This is an ongoing project that could be the perfect outlet for creative minds!

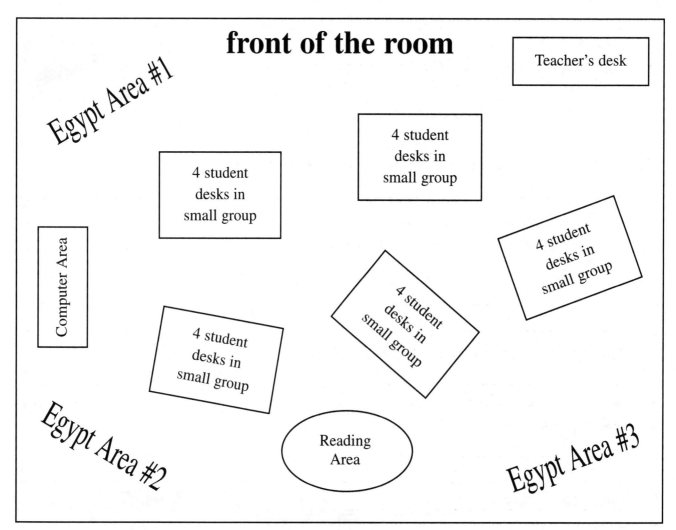

Quiz Time

1. On the back of this paper, list three main events from this section. Then, write one sentence to describe what you predict will happen in the next section.

2. Why did Melanie want to hide April's false eyelashes?

   _____

   _____

3. What did Melanie's dad say the reason was for Marshall never wanting to put down Security?

   _____

   _____

4. When the door to the Chang's apartment opened, why did April ask the girl who answered the door "if her big sister was ready for school"?

   _____

   _____

5. Who did Melanie and April decide Elizabeth looked like?

   _____

   _____

6. After a little girl was killed, many people in the neighborhood suspected the same person. Who was that person and why did people suspect him?

   _____

   _____

7. Did April, Melanie, and Elizabeth believe that person was guilty?

   _____

   _____

8. What did the kids do to occupy their time when they could not go outside to "Egypt"?

   _____

   _____

   _____

9. What was the token "sent from the mighty ones"?

   _____

10. The Egyptians said that the "air would smell of mystery as they returned to Egypt." What do you think that meant?

    _____

    _____

    _____

Create a Pharaoh

Imagine how your students will look as pharaohs and priestesses.

Each student will need a 12" x 18" (30.5 cm x 46 cm) piece of white construction paper. Using an overhead projector, trace each student's profile onto the paper. Trace only the face, not the back of their head. (See example #1.) Then, provide the students with pictures of pharaohs from the books listed in the bibliography (page 46).

The students will also need crayons, markers, and/or colored pencils to design and decorate their own Pharaoh head pieces. Students may add glitter, sequins, or other craft items. (See examples #2 and #3.) These head pieces make a great bulletin board display for open house. Don't forget to let the students trace your profile so that you can be an Egyptian along with them!

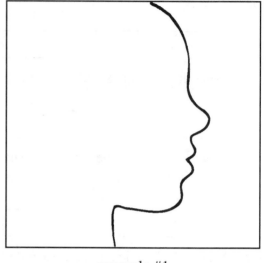

example #1

example #2

example #3

Police Report

Working with a partner on this activity, pretend that you are the investigating officers in the crime committed in the chapter, "Prisoners of Fear." After discussing the chapter, write your report below on how you think the crime happened. Use the actual events in *The Egypt Game* as your foundation and remember to include any clues you found which led to your suspicions.

Note to Teacher: Have students do this activity prior to reading the chapter, "The Hero."

Clues from the Crime	**Possible Suspects**

Police Report

Shopping for Egypt

In Chapter 6, Eyelashes and Ceremony, April suggests that they go to the Professor's store to buy the necessary items for Set and his altar, but since all they had was 50 cents, it was impossible.

Imagine that they had $50, instead. From each character's point of view, buy the items you think that he or she would have chosen but do not spend more than $50.

A-Z Antiques and Items for Egyptian Creations	
1 dozen silk flowers	$4.99
small jar of glitter	$3.79
large rubber octopus	$12.50
tape recording of Egyptian music	$9.99
clay (4 sticks per package)	$.89
beads (100-count bag)	$4.25
feathers (50-count bag)	$2.63
silk cloth (6 ft. [1.8 m] long)	$7.58
rope (12 ft. [3.7 m] long)	$2.00
plastic army men	$4.82
paints (8-color package)	$6.35
aluminum foil	$2.19
large plastic glow-in-the-dark stars	$3.50 each
rubber Halloween monster mask	$9.67
streamers	$.49
Christmas tree twinkling lights (8 ft. [2.5 m] long)	$6.80

Use the charts on the next page to shop for each character. Cut the page in half. First, choose two characters from *The Egypt Game*. Fill in the character's name at the top of each chart. Then, use the items listed above to construct "Set" and his altar the way you think that character would have done it. Write the item bought, the quantity needed, and the cost per item and then multiply the two amounts for a total cost. After you have completed the shopping for that character, add up the totals in the last column to find the total cost of the project. Remember, you cannot exceed $50. If your amount is over, or drastically under, you will need to go back and make the necessary adjustments.

Finish the activity by sketching, on separate paper, a picture of how "Set" and his altar will look with the purchased items. You will have two drawings, one for each of your characters. Before turning the project in to your teacher, attach the appropriate chart of purchased items to each drawing.

Shopping for Egypt *(cont.)*

____'s Version of "Set" and His Altar

Item	Cost	# Needed	Total

Total Cost of Project: _____

____'s Version of "Set" and His Altar

Item	Cost	# Needed	Total

Total Cost of Project: _____

Costume for an Egyptian

In Chapter 8, Prisoners of Fear, the four Egyptians begin designing Egyptian Halloween costumes because they cannot go outside to play. Now it is your turn to have some fun. In the box below, sketch a design of the Egyptian costume that you would have worn if you were a character from Zilpha Keatley Snyder's novel. You will need to include a list of materials and steps necessary to make your costume.

Your Costume Design	**Materials Needed**

Steps to Create Your Costume

Extension: Use your plans to actually create your costume. Make it small enough to display on a doll or large enough for you to model for the class!

Quiz Time

1. On the back of this paper, list three main events from this section. Then, write one sentence to describe what you predict will happen in the next section.

2. What kind of a sign was Marshall asking for?

   _____

   _____

3. Why did the Egyptian kids get stuck at every house while they were trick-or-treating?

   _____

   _____

4. What do you think Marshall meant on page 102 when he said, "Somebody already hears us"?

   _____

   _____

5. Why do you think Toby and Ken followed the Egyptians that night?

   _____

   _____

6. In the chapter, "Moods and Maybes," April receives a letter from her mom. Besides using the word "angry," list five adjectives that describe April's feelings as she read the letter.

   _____

   _____

7. Why did Toby want the group to get the hieroglyphics alphabet finished?

   _____

   _____

8. What do you think Elizabeth's reaction will be to the "Ceremony for the Dead"?

   _____

   _____

9. When Ken chose his Egyptian name, "Horemheb," there was no hieroglyph that meant "general," so he chose a picture of a sword. Can you think of another hieroglyph that would have been more suitable? Draw it in the box on the right.

10. Using the knowledge you have acquired about ancient Egyptian civilization so far, do you think it was April or Ken who was correct about the direction in which hieroglyphics were supposed to be written? Explain your reasoning.

   _____

   _____

Hieroglyphics Code

Not every hieroglyphic sign translates into our English alphabet, but this code is a close representation for hieroglyphic sound-signs. Use it to help you break the code on page 23. Students can also work in small groups to create Hieroglyphic Alphabet posters.

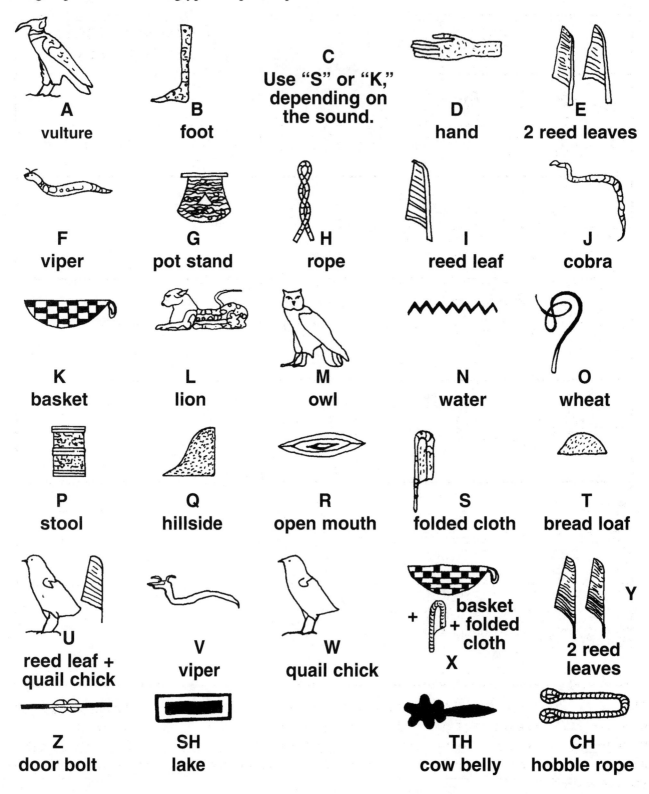

A vulture   **B** foot   **C** Use "S" or "K," depending on the sound.   **D** hand   **E** 2 reed leaves

F viper   **G** pot stand   **H** rope   **I** reed leaf   **J** cobra

K basket   **L** lion   **M** owl   **N** water   **O** wheat

P stool   **Q** hillside   **R** open mouth   **S** folded cloth   **T** bread loaf

U reed leaf + quail chick   **V** viper   **W** quail chick   **X** basket + folded cloth   **Y** 2 reed leaves

Z door bolt   **SH** lake   **TH** cow belly   **CH** hobble rope

Breaking the Code

You will need a copy of the Hieroglyphics Code (page 22) to complete this page. Each of the following words is related to a character in *The Egypt Game*. Decode the word and then write the name of the character that it describes.

Hieroglyphic	Decoded Word and Character

Now that you are familiar with these ancient alphabet symbols, it is your turn to put them to use. You will need three blank pieces of paper. Think of three words from the novel and then draw the hieroglyphic codes for each word—one word per page. Give the three pages to a classmate and have him or her decode the words and tell you how each word relates to the story. See how many classmates you can stump!

Egyptian Analogies

An analogy shows a comparison by using relationships, such as this one:

> **foot : leg :: _____ : arm**

It reads "foot is to leg as _____ is to arm." The relationship here is that a foot is the extended part of a leg, so you need to figure out what the extended part of an arm is. The answer would be "hand." To solve the comparison, first determine the relationship between the two given words and then use that relationship to find the missing word.

Directions: Complete these Egyptian analogies. Then on the line underneath, write what the relationship was that helped you find the missing word. (**Hint:** Some of these will come from *The Egypt Game*, the facts about Egypt on page 13, or other classroom reference materials.)

1. president : United States :: _____ : ancient Egypt

   _____

2. stubborn : April :: _____ : Professor

   _____

3. alphabet : America :: _____ : ancient Egypt

   _____

4. _____ April :: Mom, Dad, and Marshall : Melanie

   _____

5. cemetery : modern Egypt :: _____ : ancient Egypt

   _____

6. Toby : _____ :: Melanie : Aida

   _____

7. Mississippi River : USA :: _____ : Egypt

   _____

8. April : Melanie :: _____ : Marshall

   _____

9. _____ : USA :: papyrus : ancient Egypt

   _____

Note to Teacher: Consider using the page as a partner activity since analogies can be difficult for some students.

Hieroglyph Necklaces

Many people have jewelry, especially necklaces, that spell their names. In this activity, students will make their own "personal" necklaces—Egyptian style!

Prior to presenting this activity, enlarge the shape and trace it several times onto tagboard for students to use as patterns. Students will trace the shape and then use the Hieroglyphics Code on page 22 to spell their own names. These necklaces can easily be turned into a learning center after the students finish spelling their names. Use yarn to hang the necklaces from a window or bulletin board, along with a Code Page. During the students' free time, they can see how many of their classmates' names they can decode. Students can also choose an Egyptian name to translate into hieroglyphs. Have the necklaces available at open house for parents to decode, too!

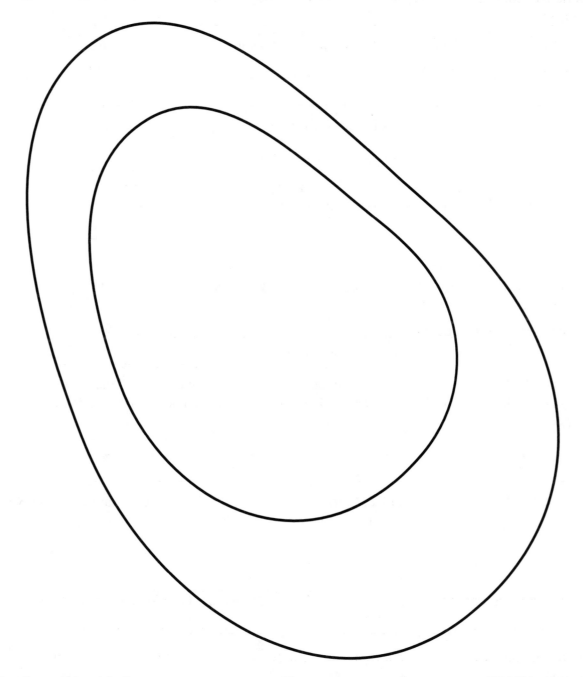

Quiz Time

1. On the back of this paper, list three main events from this section. Then, write one sentence to describe what you predict will happen in the next section.

2. In this section, the kids tell how long an actual mummification process and funeral ceremony took. How long did they say it was?

   _____

   _____

3. Who planned the steps for the burial of Pete-ho-tep?

   _____

   _____

4. Why did they put birdseed and Petey's favorite toys in the pyramid with the dead bird?

   _____

   _____

5. Who got to write the first question for the oracle?

   _____

   _____

6. Where did they place the question for the oracle?

   _____

   _____

7. Name the two reasons why they were anxious to get back to Egypt after Ken's question was answered?

   _____

   _____

8. When Melanie read the question April had written to the oracle, she said that is was the same question that she thought it would be. How do you think she knew what question April would ask?

   _____

   _____

9. At the end of the chapter entitled, "Where's Security?," the last sentence says that Toby was the most worried of all. Why do you think he was worried?

   _____

   _____

10. Who do you think answered the question about Security and put him under Set's throne?

    _____

    _____

A Lost Friend

At the end of the chapter entitled, "Where is Security?," the Egyptians don't know if Marshall will ever find his octopus again. Imagine that when you were four years old, you went through the same experience; a special friend—toy or blanket—was lost and never found again. Pretending that Security is not found, write a letter to Marshall explaining to him how you felt when you had lost your special friend and how you dealt with it.

Dear Marshall,

Questions for the Oracle

The purpose of the oracle in the ancient Egyptian civilization was to give advice and direction about the future. Cut out the strips below. On each one, write a question you have about the future, such as "Will I pass the test on *The Egypt Game*?" Then trade strips with a classmate. You will become the oracle for his questions, and he will become the oracle for yours. Your task is to be wise and knowledgeable as you answer each question the way an oracle would answer. Then return the strips to each other and check out your future!

To Ask or Not?

In the chapter called "The Oracle of Thoth," the Egyptians wrote questions to ask the oracle. In the English language, there are three main types of sentences, each of them using a specific type of punctuation mark.

- A *declarative sentence* makes a statement and uses a period (.).

- An *interrogative sentence* asks a question and uses a question mark (?).

- An *exclamatory sentence* expresses strong emotion and uses an exclamation mark (!).

Directions: Identify what types of sentences are listed below by writing a D for declarative, I for interrogative, or E for exclamatory in the space provided. Add the correct ending punctuation. Note that in sentences 10 and 15, the punctuation mark will go inside of the quotation marks.

_____ 1. Marshall seemed content to sit and listen

_____ 2. Who does Elizabeth look like

_____ 3. It was a terrible and shocking thing

_____ 4. Hey, what are you two supposed to be

_____ 5. Before April knew what was happening, someone grabbed her from behind

_____ 6. Ken and Toby were the most disgusting boys in the world

_____ 7. Let the Great Ceremony of the Celebration of the Return to Egypt begin

_____ 8. April waited and waited for a phone call from her mom, but it never came

_____ 9. Everybody liked Melanie's name and hieroglyph

_____10. "Look," April gasped, "a shooting star "

_____11. What do you mean, somebody already heard us

_____12. The Crocodile God declared that Security must be sacrificed

_____13. That afternoon was spent discussing oracles

_____14. Could we pull out some hairs or cut off some fingernails

_____15. April screamed, "You boys are just awful "

Ceremony Sequence

Toby had many ideas about how he envisioned the "Ceremony for the Dead." Below are his ideas, plus those of the other Egyptians. Number them in the correct order in which they occurred in the book as the kids prepared Pete-ho-tep's body for burial.

_____ Wrap Pete-ho-tep in oil-soaked clothes.

_____ Egyptians sprinkle ashes on their heads and wail.

_____ Prepare a saltwater bath for the bird.

_____ Gather needed items for mummification.

_____ Egyptians march around the altar and beat their chests.

_____ Lay Pete-ho-tep to rest in a pyramid filled with birdseed.

_____ Research ideas on how to make a mummy.

_____ Anoint Pete-ho-tep with spices and perfumes.

_____ Toby calls Egyptians with a list of necessary supplies.

_____ Soak the bird in brine (saltwater).

Now think of something you do on a regular basis that has several steps involved, such as your morning routine before school, preparing dinner, etc. Below, and on the back of this page, write out one of those sequences. Start with the first thing you do, then the next, etc., until you have the activity completed. You will be amazed at how many steps it takes to complete your daily routines. Then cross out one of those steps and imagine how the activity would be if this step were omitted or if the steps were done in the wrong order!

_____

_____

_____

_____

_____

Quiz Time

1. On the back of this page, list three main events from this section.

2. Why didn't Marshall like people to say "baby-sitter"?

    _____

    _____

3. Why do you think Marshall did not yell for help?

    _____

    _____

4. When the inspector said that the Professor could not give an alibi for the other times, what did he mean?

    _____

    _____

5. At the end of the chapter called "The Hero," Marshall decides he does not need to carry Security around much anymore. Why do you think he made that decision?

    _____

    _____

6. Why did all the neighbors start shopping at the Professor's shop?

    _____

    _____

7. Why do you think April told her mom that she could not come for Christmas?

    _____

    _____

8. In the last chapter, the Professor calls himself a "dusty junkyard." This kind of comparison is called a *metaphor*. Explain what you think this metaphor means.

    _____

    _____

9. Why did the Professor write the answer to the last question to the oracle?

    _____

    _____

10. When the kids go back to Egypt after Christmas, do you think things will be the same or different from before? Explain your reasoning.

    _____

    _____

Egyptian Vocabulary Guessing Game

Below are several words from Egyptian civilizations. Some of these were mentioned in the novel, while others will be new to you. In this activity, you will make vocabulary illustration cards to play a guessing game.

To Prepare the Cards:

1. Read over all of the words and definitions.
2. Choose ten words that are most interesting to you.
3. Gather a set of 10 large, blank cards (8 ½ " x 11" [22 cm x 28 cm] sheets of white construction paper work well).

To Play the Game:

1. Choose a partner.
2. Show your partner your illustrations, one at a time, and see if he/she can guess the definition.
3. Then reverse roles and play the game again.

4. On each card, write one of the definitions until you have a different definition on each of the ten cards.
5. Turn all of the cards over to the blank side and write the appropriate word in the top right-hand corner.
6. Create an illustration that shows the meaning of the word. The illustration could be a picture of the real definition or a play on words that tells the definition.

Words from Ancient Egypt

amulet – a charm worn by the living or placed on a mummy to ward off evil spirits and to bring good luck

anthropoid – coffin in the shape of a human

Ba – believed by ancient Egyptians to be the spirit or soul. It is often depicted as a bird with a human head.

Book of the Dead – a collection of spells to help the dead reach the next life safely

canopic jars – a set of jars used in mummification that held the internal organs such as the brain, intestines, and liver

cartouche – an oval that was drawn to contain the hieroglyphs that spelled the king or queen's name

coffin – a container for a mummy

Egyptologist – an archaeologist who studies ancient Egypt

hieroglyphs – ancient Egyptian writing that used symbols usually based on animals, humans, and gods

mastaba – part of a tomb above the ground that looked like a bench

mummy – preserved body of a dead person or animal

natron – a salt used in mummification

Necropolis – Egyptian burial grounds, or "city of the dead"

memes – a striped headcloth worn by the Pharaoh

nilometer – a staircase found in temples that was next to the Nile

papyrus – a water reed used to make paper in ancient Egypt

Pharaoh – the Egyptian king, his name means "Great House"

sarcophagus – a stone container for the coffin and the mummy

Sphinx – a statue in the shape of a lion with the head of a human or ram

uraeus – a cobra emblem worn by the Pharaoh as part of the headdress

Imagine That!

In *The Egypt Game*, April and Melanie enjoy playing what they call "imagining games." Once they find the yard they call "Egypt," they begin an imagining game that becomes a part of their daily lives.

Now it's your turn to use your imagination. With a partner, you will create a concrete version of *The Egypt Game* in the form of a board game. Your game will be based on events in the novel. Use the game board sample below to give you an idea on how to begin. Follow these directions to make your game:

1. Decide the shape of your game board and what the object of the game will be.

2. Sketch your game board out on scratch paper. Use your imagination! Think beyond just rolling the dice and moving the designated number of spaces.

3. Create your game's playing pieces and a list of rules and instructions for the game. Make sure your rules and instructions provide simple, step-by-step directions on how to play the game.

4. Make a set of game cards with questions from *The Egypt Game* to be used in your board game. Write each question on its own 3" x 5" (8 cm x 13 cm) card. On the back of each card, write down the answer to each question and the name of the chapter where the answer can be found. (Your list of rules will tell how the questions will be used in the game.)

5. Use your sketch as your guide as you make your actual game board.

6. As you read your rules and instruction page, practice playing your game with your partner to make sure that everything is clear, understandable, and that your game actually works.

7. On the day that your teacher assigns as "Egypt Game Day," trade games with another pair of students. You and your partner will have the opportunity to play someone else's Egypt Game, while they play yours!

Extension: Choose five of the questions from your game and give them to your teacher. These can be your suggested questions for a test on *The Egypt Game*. You may see your own questions on the test!

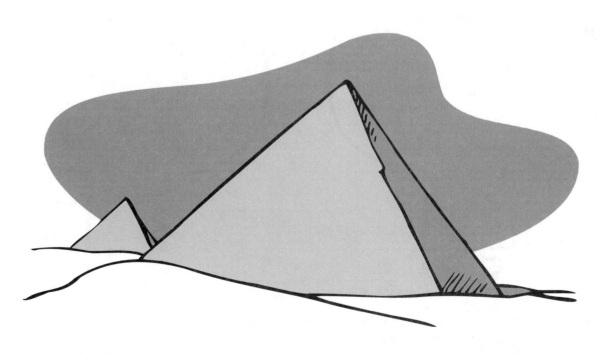

Key Clues

In *The Egypt Game*, the keys the Professor gave the children would lead them back to Egypt. Use the clues on each of the keys below to find out what number they lead you to. Write the answer at the bottom of the key.

1. I am a multiple of 5.
   I am less than 100.
   I am more than 75.
   I am divisible by 4.
   What number am I?

2. I am an odd number.
   I am greater than 5 x 12.
   But I am less than 7 x 10.
   I am divisible by 3.
   I am not divisible by 9.
   What number am I?

3. I am an even number.
   I am greater than 12 x 11.
   I am less than 12 x 13.
   I am not divisible by 10.
   I am divisible by 3 but not 12.
   What number am I?

4. I am less than 20 dozen.
   I am more than 5 x 46.
   I am only divisible by 1 and myself, but I am not the number 233.
   What number am I?

Now create two number puzzles on your own. Be sure to give an answer. You may see one of your own number puzzles on the next math test!

Pyramid Internet Research

The pyramids in Egypt are one of the ways we have been able to learn about the ancient Egyptian civilizations and how they lived. Research the Great Pyramid on the Internet.

When you arrive at this site, use the arrow on the right side of the screen to scroll down the page and find answers to the following questions. When you have finished your research, turn this paper over and, using classroom resources, information from class discussions, and knowledge you have acquired during your study of Egypt, decide whether you are in agreement with the facts presented by the Web site. One of the most important parts of Internet research is the tool of evaluation, the ability to filter through a site to find the real facts. Write a short summary of your opinion of this site and be sure to include how accurate you think it is.

Answer the following according to the information found on the Web site.

1. Who built the pyramids? _____

2. Why were these tombs needed? _____

   _____

3. The pyramids are _____ times as big as the Empire State Building in New York City.

4. The Great Pyramid is considered to be one of the Seven Wonders of the Ancient World. Which of these wonders are still in existence today?

   _____

5. What direction does the pyramid face? _____

6. What is the size of the Great Pyramid's base? _____

7. In relationship to the earth's land mass, where is the Great Pyramid located?

   _____

8. From what type of rock is most of the pyramid constructed?

   _____

9. Within the Great Pyramid, how many bodies and pieces of treasure were found?

   _____

10. The Great Pyramid is visible from a great distance because of its massive size. Name two distant places from where you can see the pyramid.

    _____

    _____

Newbery Award Winners

The Newbery Medal Award Books and Newbery Honor Books are named after John Newbery, the famous 18th century publisher of children's books in England. These prestigious awards were first given in 1921 and have come to represent the very best in children's literature. *The Egypt Game* won the award of Newbery Honor Book in 1968. Below is a list of other Newbery Medal winners and Newbery Honor Books. Not only are these great assets for your classroom library, but they could lead to many activities, such as a study of the winning books to look for similarities and differences. You could also introduce your students to the Newbery Medal home page on the Internet at the following address:

http://www.ala.org/alsc/newbery.html

This site lists all the past winners for each year and talks about the criteria for selection. After the class finishes reading *The Egypt Game*, have the students research the Newbery Web site and then choose another award book to read. Each student should choose a different book and then do a presentation on that book to introduce it to the rest of the class.

Other Newbery Honor books by Zilpha Keatley Snyder:

The Headless Cupid

The Witches of Worm

Other Newbery winners:

The Black Cauldron by Lloyd Alexander

The Midwife's Apprentice by Karen Cushman

The Door in the Wall by Marguerite de Angeli

Johnny Tremain by Esther Forbes

Homesick: My Own Story by Jean Fritz

Lily's Crossing by Patricia Reilly Giff

From the Mixed-up Files of Mrs. Basil E. Frankweiler by E. L. Konigsburg

A Wrinkle in Time by Madeleine L'Engle

Number the Stars by Lois Lowry

Sarah, Plain and Tall by Patricia MacLachlan

Island of the Blue Dolphins by Scott O'Dell

The Winter Room by Gary Paulsen

Shiloh by Phyllis Reynolds Naylor

The Sign of the Beaver by Elizabeth George Speare

The Witch of Blackbird Pond by Elizabeth George Speare

Dragon's Gate by Laurence Yep

Book Report Ideas

There are many ways to report on a book you have read. After you have finished reading *The Egypt Game*, choose one method of reporting on the book. It may be a particular style that your teacher suggests or he or she may ask you to choose from the ideas below.

- **Book in a Bag**

   This report is given using a brown grocery sack. Think about how a recipe needs certain ingredients. These are similar to the "ingredients" of a novel. Your "ingredients" could be glued to empty food containers or mounted on tagboard reproductions, such as a drawing of a can of corn. Now decide on your ingredients. These could be characters, setting, plot, conflict, as well as others you choose. You will pull each item out of your grocery sack as you present your report and tell how that item contributed to the novel.

- **Letter to the Author**

   This report is given by writing a letter to Zilpha Keatley Snyder. You will tell her your opinion of *The Egypt Game* and you will include any questions you have about the story. You can include favorite sections or even changes you might make to the story, or a character you may want to add. Also, include your suggestions for a new novel entitled, *The Egypt Game Continues*.

- **Ad Campaign**

   In the same way that an ad company tries to sell a product, you will try and "sell" *The Egypt Game*. Make arrangements to give your report to another class. Your job will be to convince them to read the book. Your presentation could be a commercial, a poster representing a simulated billboard, or even a jingle. Be persuasive!

- **Who's Who?**

   This report describes the characters from *The Egypt Game*. Choose your favorite characters from the story. Then use a piece of poster board to create your own pyramid. (Remember, it has a square base with four triangular sides.) On each side of the pyramid, you will describe that character. Your description could be in the form of a poem, a short biographical report, or any other way you choose. After all four sides are done, assemble your pyramid using tape or glue. As you present your report, turn the pyramid as you discuss the character.

- **One-Act Play**

   With a group of students, rewrite one of the chapters of *The Egypt Game* into a short play. Practice the play and act it out in front of the class. Remember to read your lines with feeling and how you envision that the characters would speak. And don't forget the costumes and the props!

- **What Happens Next?**

   Write a sequel to *The Egypt Game*, using the same characters from the story and perhaps adding a new one. Try to write in the style of the author and include things that the original characters in the story would do.

Research Ideas

Describe three things you read in *The Egypt Game* that you would like to learn more about.

1. _____

_____

2. _____

_____

3. _____

_____

Work individually or in a group to research one or more of the areas that you named above or one of the things listed below. Be prepared to share your findings with the rest of the class in an oral presentation.

Mysteries of Egypt	Famous People in Egypt's History
The Sphinx	King Akhenaten
The Nile River	King Khufu
The Pyramids	King Ramses
Mummification	King Sneferu
Nubian Civilization	King Thutmose III
Rosetta Stone	King Tutankhamen
Papyrus	Imhotep
Valley of the Kings	Moses
Headdresses or Crowns	Queen Cleopatra
Egyptian Gods	Queen Hatshepsut
Religious Festivals	Queen Hetepheres
Polytheism	Queen Nefertiti
Pottery	
Egyptian Art/Painting	
Simple Machines of the Period	
Trade	

Culminating Books

As a culminating project for *The Egypt Game,* direct the students to make a book. Present them with both options below and let them choose one to complete or assign each pair or group a specific idea.

Flap Book

Materials: pencil; wide marking pen; construction paper or tagboard; writing paper; stapler

Directions:

- Have the students draw an Egyptian shape—a hippo, the outline of the Sphinx, Nefertiti's head, etc.
- For more stability glue the shape to construction paper, tagboard, or other heavy paper; cut out around the outline.
- With the marking pen, draw a wide outline along the edge of the shape.
- Cut out paper rectangles or squares that will fit inside the shape. Use these for writing the story.
- When the writing has been completed, place the rectangles one on top of each other in correct story order. Staple to the body of the shape.
- Add details to the shape, if desired.

Writing Topics

- On each page write a different mysterious event from *The Egypt Game.*
- Draw a story map of the plot; include characters, conflict, climax, and resolution.

Multi-Flap Book

Materials: oaktag or poster board; cardboard (a side cut from a box); craft knife or box cutter; glue; fine-line marking pens; pencil; ruler.

Directions:

- Fold a sheet of oaktag or poster board in half.
- Draw a shape outline, keeping one edge on the fold.
- Keep folded and cut out; lay it flat on the cardboard on a flat surface.
- With a pencil and ruler, lightly draw squares on the body of the shape that is on the right side.
- Cut along the bottom and two sides only of each square; fold up.
- Fold the shape together so the flaps are facing out and up.
- Glue the two shapes together by placing a line of glue along the edge (or outline). Do not glue the area behind the flaps.
- Use the marking pens to write on and underneath each flap (See suggestions below.); add details to the shape, if desired.

Writing Topics

- Write a question about a character on the flap; write the answer in the space behind the flap. For example: Who witnessed the Egypt Game from afar? (*The Professor*)
- On the top flap, write a definition. Behind it write the words. Use vocabulary from *The Egypt Game.*

Follow-Ups

Once students have completed reading *The Egypt Game*, follow it up with any of the activities on this page. For more effective projects, allow students to choose an activity which interests them.

- Read another mystery story. (Suggestions: Take the students on a field trip to a local library so a children's librarian can provide information on age-appropriate mystery books, or ask students to compare *The Egypt Game* to some of the other mysteries written by Zilpha Keatley Snyder.)

- Convince others to read the book by reading a few paragraphs aloud to them—but don't give away the ending!

- Stamp a message with the Metropolitan Museum of Art's Hieroglyphic Stamp Set and Fun with Hieroglyphics Stationery (the stationery includes colorful stickers). Both are available at book stores and teacher supply stores.

- Display a copy of Paul Klee's painting *Sinbad the Sailor*. It was inspired by a trip he made down the Nile River. Paint an Egyptian picture using squares. With colored pencils or markers, color the squares of 1-inch (2.54 cm) graph paper using various bright colors. Then draw a picture over the background using a black marker. Create a title for your art work.

- Read *The Egyptian Cinderella* by Shirley Climo (Harper, 1989) or *The Prince Who Knew His Fate* by Lise Manniche (Putnam, 1982). Write your own Egyptian fairy tale based on what you know about ancient Egyptian beliefs.

- Build a giant pyramid from appliance boxes. Tape the edges together with duct tape or electrical tape. Cut an opening on one side for entry. Use it as a private reading room, "think tank," or creative writing center. For more complete directions, see *The Pyramids* by Harriette Abels (Crestwood House, 1987).

- Create a system of hieroglyphs. Write a short story on 3" x 5" (8 cm x 13 cm) index cards. Staple cards together at the left side. Now write the same story using your hieroglyph system. Staple those cards together. Attach both stories, one above the other, to a cardboard or tagboard background.

- Use a Styrofoam head base (used to hold wigs; available in beauty supply stores) or make one out of papier mâché. Apply make-up to resemble Cleopatra or Nefertiti. Make a paper or yarn wig. Or, draw an oval on an 8 1/2" x 11" (22 cm x 28 cm) sheet of white paper. With make-up draw the features of an Egyptian princess.

Nefertiti and Cleopatra

In *The Egypt Game*, April and Melanie observe that Elizabeth bears a strong resemblance to Nefertiti so she is given the role of Queen Neferbeth in their imaginative game. If Elizabeth had resembled Cleopatra, she might have been given the name Cleobeth.

Just who were Nefertiti and Cleopatra? Research both of these famous Egyptian women. Then read the sentences below. Circle N if the statement applies to Nefertiti. Circle C if the statement applies to Cleopatra.

1. N C She was thought to be the mother-in-law of Tutankhamen.
2. N C She was a descendant of the Ptolemies, a Greek family.
3. N C She committed suicide by allowing herself to be bitten by an asp.
4. N C Her brother exiled her so he could become the sole ruler of Egypt.
5. N C The statue of her head is world famous.
6. N C She had one son.
7. N C Her husband was the pharaoh Amenhotep IV.
8. N C She had six daughters.
9. N C She rolled herself up into a rug as a gift for Caesar.
10. N C Mark Anthony planned to make her his queen.
11. N C Her husband changed his name to Akhenaten in honor of the sun god Aten.
12. N C The Romans distrusted her.
13. N C Her daughter Ankhesenamen was thought to be the wife of Tutankhamen.
14. N C Her second child died in infancy.
15. N C Caesar helped her regain the throne in Egypt.

Activities

- You are a reporter for the *Roman Times*. You have just learned that Mark Anthony has attempted to commit suicide and is being carried to Cleopatra. Write a new article about the events leading up to this incident and report its outcome.
- Write an appropriate obituary for Cleopatra.
- Cleopatra's romance with Mark Anthony is legendary. Name some other famous historical couples. Name some famous fictional couples.
- Research another famous female leader such as Golda Meir (Israel), Margaret Thatcher (Great Britain), Queen Isabella (Spain), etc. Write a brief report about their accomplishments.
- Compare Nefertiti and Cleopatra in a Venn diagram.
- Choose one of these titles and write a story: *The Greatest Love Story Ever Told; Web of Lies; How to Look Like Cleopatra; How to Become Queen of Egypt.*
- If you could meet Cleopatra today, what are five questions you would like to ask her? Write an interview you would conduct with her and then supply her with the answers.

Meet the Author

Would you have guessed that Zilpha Keatly Snyder was once a public school teacher or that all six of the main characters in *The Egypt Game* were based on real children that she'd once taught? Uncover more interesting facts about Ms. Snyder and her career in the newspaper article below.

The Author's Gazette

Who:　Zilpha Keatley Snyder was born May 11, 1927, in Lemoore, California. She married Larry Alan Snyder in 1950 and has one daughter and two sons. She graduated from Whittier College and also studied at the University of California, Berkeley.

What:　Ms. Snyder began her career as a school teacher and taught upper grades for nine years in California, New York, Washington, and Alaska. She then switched to writing but credits her teaching experience as invaluable to her writing. As she explained, her students provided her with ideas, personalities, and language which she was able to incorporate into her writings.

Where:　Zilpha Keatley Snyder now lives with her husband in a northern California town close to San Francisco.

When:　In 1964, *Season of Ponies* won an ALA Notable Book award.

In 1965, *The Velvet Room* was placed on the Horn Book honor list.

In 1967, *The Egypt Game* received an ALA Notable Book award and was on the Horn Book honor list.

Why:　Zilpha explains that she writes because she realized at an early age that writing is what she wanted to do. Her love of books grew out of the fact that during her childhood there wasn't much money—it was the Depression and World War II era. She turned to books and read nearly one a day throughout those early years.

How:　How can you find out more about Zilpha Keatley Snyder? Look in the reference section of the library for a series of books entitled *Something About the Author*.

Extension: Write an interview you would like to have with this author.

Unit Test

Matching: Match the character with his or her description.

_____ 1. April   a. her pet died

_____ 2. Melanie   b. owned yard where "Egypt" was

_____ 3. Marshall   c. April's best friend

_____ 4. Elizabeth   d. Egyptian name was Horemheb

_____ 5. Professor   e. the youngest Egyptian

_____ 6. Ken   f. wrote answers to the first oracle questions

_____ 7. Toby   g. liked to wear false eyelashes

True or False: Write true or false next to each statement.

_____ 1. Security was the name of Elizabeth's pet bird.

_____ 2. Ken and Toby discovered Egypt on Halloween night.

_____ 3. Melanie had one brother.

_____ 4. The Professor was a teacher at Melanie's school.

_____ 5. Marshall saw the person who grabbed April.

_____ 6. Elizabeth was older than April and Melanie.

_____ 7. Ken enjoyed all of the ceremonies they did in Egypt.

_____ 8. Toby called April "February."

_____ 9. The Egypt Game was a board game the kids played after school.

_____ 10. The Professor was guilty of the murder.

Short Answer: Respond to the following questions.

_____ 1. Who were the original Egyptians in the game?

_____ 2. What kind of an animal was Thoth?

_____ 3. What job did Marshall get to have in Egypt?

_____ 4. Who found "Security" when he was lost?

Essay: Respond to the following in detail on the back of this page.

1. Describe why April is living with her grandmother at Casa Rosada and how she feels about the situation.

2. If the Professor had not given the kids the keys to get back into Egypt, explain how they could have continued the game.

Responses

Directions: Explain the meaning and significance of each of these quotations from The Egypt Game.

Chapter 2 : *"Dorothea always said, 'I'll take mine new and shiny.' "*

Chapter 3 : *"Actually Melanie knew that April was showboating . . . ."*

Chapter 5 : *"It wasn't long afterwards that the curtain on the small window at the back of the Professor's store was pushed very carefully to one side."*

Chapter 6 : *"Feeling triumphant and treacherous at the same time, Melanie took the eyelashes home and hid them in her closet."*

Chapter 8 : *"She'd noticed before that April, in spite of her sophisticated ways, really didn't know much at all about certain kinds of things."*

Chapter 9 : *"It occurred to Melanie that it was the first time she'd ever seen April smile at her grandmother."*

Chapter 11 : *"The figure teetered wildly in the dim light, and then sprang forward to land in a horrible threatening crouch, right in the middle of Egypt."*

Chapter 12 : *" 'What are we going to do?' April said finally. 'We just can't play the Egypt Game with those—those—boys there.'"*

Chapter 15 : *"But they needn't have wondered. The boys took part, all right, and to an extent that nobody had expected."*

Chapter 19 : *"When it came to conducting ceremonies, Ken and Elizabeth were definitely the spectator type."*

Note to Teacher: Choose an appropriate number of quotes for your students.

Conversations

Directions: Work with a partner to perform the conversations that might have occurred in each of the following situations.

- April and her mother before April had to move to her grandmother's apartment

- April's mom and her grandmother as they decide what to do with April

- The Professor, April, and Melanie as the girls ask his permission to use the yard

- Melanie and April, if one of them wanted Elizabeth to join the game, but the other did not

- Melanie and Marshall as she tries to convince him to leave Security at home

- Ken and Toby before they invaded Egypt on Halloween night

- Marshall and the inspector if Marshall would have actually talked to him

- The Egyptians and the trick-or-treating group if the parents had noticed the kids were missing

- April and her mom after Christmas when her mom asked her to move back home

- Melanie and her parents as she tells them about Egypt and the new keys

- Ken, Toby, and a group of their friends as they tell them they don't want to play on the winter basketball league because of a "prior commitment"

Extension: Perform one of your conversation ideas for the characters in *The Egypt Game*. Write your conversation ideas on the lines below.

_____

_____

_____

_____

_____

_____

_____

_____

_____

_____

_____

_____

Bibliography of Related Resources

Related Books

Aliki. *Mummies Made in Egypt*. HarperCollins Children's Books, 1985.

David, Rosalie. *Growing Up in Ancient Egypt*. Larousse Kingfisher Chambers, Inc., 1998.

Giblin, James. *The Riddle of the Rosetta Stone: Key to Ancient Egypt*. HarperCollins, 1993.

Green, Roger Lancelyn. *Tales of Ancient Egypt*. Viking Penguin, 1996.

Greenburg, Dan. *Never Trust a Cat Who Wears Earrings*. Putnam, 1997.

Macauley, David. *Pyramid*. Houghton Mifflin, 1977.

Morley, Jacqueline. *How Would You Survive as an Egyptian?* Franklin Watts, 1996.

Payne, Elizabeth Ann. *The Pharaohs of Ancient Egypt*. Alfred A. Knopf Books for Young Readers, 1998.

Perl, Lila. *Mummies, Tombs, and Treasure*. Houghton Mifflin, 1990.

Putnam, James. *Pyramid: Eyewitness Books*. Dorling Kindersley Publishing, Inc., 2000.

Rubalcaba, Jill. *A Place in the Sun*. Penguin Putnam, 1998.

Scieszka, Jon. *Tut, Tut*. Penguin Putnam, Inc., 1998.

Stanley, Diane. *Cleopatra*. Morrow, William and Co., 1997.

Steele, Philip. *The Best Book of Mummies*. Larousee Kingfisher Chambers, Inc., 1998.

Trumble, Kelly. *Cat Mummies*. Houghton Mifflin, 1999.

Yolen, Jane. *The Prince of Egypt*. Penguin Putnam, 1998.

Movies/Videos

Pyramids: Secrets of the Unknown (30 minutes)

Egypt, from the Rand McNally "Video Traveller Collection" (35 minutes)

Egypt: A Gift to Civilization (90 minutes)

Rosetta Stone (50 minutes)

Hieroglyphs (50 minutes)

An A & E Biography, *Cleopatra: Destiny's Queen* (50 minutes)

Video Visits: Egypt (58 minutes)

King Tut: Tomb of Treasure (25 minutes)

Tut: Boy King, is an NBC News Special that runs for 60 minutes, narrated by Orson Welles.

CD-ROM

The Road to Ancient Egypt CD-ROM

Everyday Life in Ancient Egypt CD-ROM

The National Geographic "Ancient Civilizations" series includes a Picture Pack set and *Ancient Egypt* CD-ROM.

Nile: Passage to Egypt CD-ROM is an offering of the Discovery Channel.

The "Ancient History CD-ROM series" offers *Ancient Egyptians*.

"The Road to Ancient Civilizations CD-ROM" series has *The Road to Ancient Egypt*.

"Thematic Literature Connections: The Ancient World CD-ROMS" puts together student and teacher guides plus maps and time lines, glossaries, anagrams, puzzles, educational games, worksheets, assignments, and *Life in Ancient Egypt* CD-ROM.

Ancient History series, *Ancient Egyptians* CD-ROM

Ancient Origins CD-ROM is an offering of 5 million years of human development that covers 44 different cultures.

Answer Key

page 10

1. Answers will vary.
2. Answers will vary.
3. April found a book about Egyptian pharaohs.
4. No one knew about him. He was mysterious.
5. Answers will vary.
6. They began in August.
7. Answers will vary.
8. They lived in Casa Rosada.
9. They told him he could be a king.
10. It was 2,000 years old.

page 11

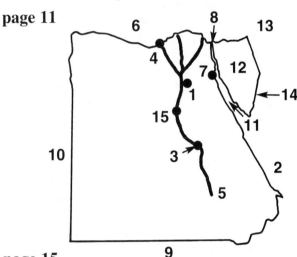

page 15

1. Answers will vary.
2. She wanted to help April be accepted by the other kids at school.
3. He said that Marshall did not like being a baby; that it offended his dignity.
4. It was because Elizabeth was so small.
5. She looked like Nefertiti.
6. They suspected the Professor because he was so mysterious.
7. No, they did not believe it.
8. They made Egyptian costumes.
9. The sign was an old pigeon feather.
10. Answers will vary.

page 21

1. Answers will vary.
2. He wanted a sign used in a demonstration.

3. Their costumes were so unique and everyone wanted to see them.
4. Answers will vary.
5. Answers will vary.
6. Answers will vary.
7. It was so that they could pass coded notes at school.
8. Answers will vary.
9. Answers will vary.
10. Answers will vary

Page 23

Sheesh; Ken

Dorothea; April

Box man; Toby

Nefertiti; Elizabeth

Security; Marshall

Paper Dolls; Melanie

Page 24

1. Pharaoh; leader of the country
2. Answers will vary; words to describe the character
3. Hieroglyphics; symbols used in writing
4. Grandma; who she lives with
5. Pyramid; where the dead are buried
6. Ramose; Egyptian name
7. Nile River; major river in the country
8. Security; best friend
9. Trees; substance paper is made from

Page 26

1. Answers will vary.
2. The process took 40 days.
3. Toby planned the burial.
4. He would need them in the afterlife.
5. Ken got to ask the first one.
6. The question was in Thoth's beak.
7. They wanted to see if April's question would be answered and if they could find Security.
8. Answers will vary.
9. Answers will vary.
10. Answers will vary.

Answer Key *(cont.)*

Page 29

1. D.
2. I ?
3. E !
4. I ?
5. D.
6. D.
7. E !
8. D.
9. D.
10. E !
11. I ?
12. E.
13. D.
14. I ?
15. E !

Page 30

9, 2, 6, 5, 1, 10, 3, 8, 4, 7

Page 31

1. Answers will vary.
2. He did not consider himself to be a baby. It insulted his dignity.
3. Answers will vary.
4. It means the Professor could not say where he was at those times or that no one could confirm his story.
5. Answers will vary.
6. They wanted to make up for the things they thought and said about him.
7. Answers will vary.
8. He meant things had collected all around him, never cleaned out or used.
9. He wanted to help them find where he put Security.
10. Answers will vary.

Page 34

1. 80
2. 69
3. 138
4. 239

Page 35

1. It took armies of slaves.
2. They wanted to preserve the Pharaoh's royal body for the after-life.
3. It is 30 times as big.
4. Only the Pyramid is left.

5. It faces true north.
6. The base is 13.6 acres.
7. It was built at the exact center of the earth.
8. The rocks are limestone.
9. None were found.
10. You can see it from the moon and Israel.

Page 41

1. N
2. C
3. C
4. C
5. N
6. C
7. N
8. N
9. C
10. C
11. N
12. C
13. N
14. N
15. C

Page 43

Matching

1. G
2. C
3. E
4. A
5. B
6. D
7. F

True or False

1. false
2. true
3. true
4. false
5. true
6. false
7. false
8. true
9. false
10. false

Short Answer:

1. Melanie, April, and Marshall
2. an owl
3. a junior Pharaoh
4. the Professor

Essay: Answers will vary.